Pleasure

VantagePoint Books

A Ministry of
THE CHRISTIAN COUNSELING &
EDUCATIONAL FOUNDATION
Glenside, Pennsylvania

VantagePoint Books
Susan Lutz, Editor

Pleasure

David Powlison

3143 S. Stratford Road, Winston-Salem, NC 27103-5825
www.punchbookstore.com

© 2005 by David Powlison

Printed in the United States of America.

Library of Congress Cataloging-in-Publication Data

ISBN 0-9762308-6-0

How do you feel about pleasure? In a culture that is in love with recreation, entertainment, and amusement, this is one of life's most important questions. Unfortunately, few of us ask it. We are too easily enticed by the endless array of distractions our culture so willingly supplies. When we do stop to consider the question, it can be downright depressing. Neil Postman, for example, says that we are "amusing ourselves to death." He cautions that we are losing our independence, maturity, and history as we are swallowed up in the pursuit of pleasure. He fears that "what we love will ruin us," as truth is "drowned in a sea of irrelevance."[1] Is he right?

How do *you* feel about pleasure? If you agree with Postman, what should we do? Flannery O'Connor once described a Christian's task like this: "Push back against the age as hard as it pushes against you." She was not someone who wanted to withdraw from her world. She was not ranting against culture. We push against culture by entering into it, by saying, "This is not *their* culture. This is *our* culture, the stage on which we are called to live." If we live in an age obsessed with pleasure, the way we push against the darkness is to enter it, bringing brighter and better joys, more lasting and truer pleasures, by thinking biblically about pleasure and communicating to people what real pleasure is.

WHAT IS TRUE PLEASURE?

We must begin by admitting that Christians often have a problem with pleasure. We tend to be shocked by hedonism; it is a reckless, self-indulgent impulse that depresses, irritates – and tempts us. We see people who *are* literally amusing themselves to death and we often react by going in the other direction, towards a stoic denial of feeling. We tend to demean pleasure and distrust it, as if the Christian life is to be lived despite what we feel. We convey the idea that pleasure and joy may be automatically evil. They are certainly irrelevant. They don't really count. We end up focusing on the sphere of the intellect and the will – true and false, right and wrong, sin and morality.

These are all things we should be concerned about. But that doesn't mean we should ignore the fact that God also made us to feel. Something is missing if we don't ask questions about what is beautiful, about joy and sorrow, pleasure and pain, adoration and disgust.

Some people attempt to bridge the gap by saying (correctly) that the Christian life is a wonderful union between duty and desire. But too often, our rationalistic bias leads us to hear this as: "Do what you are supposed to and, by the way, enjoy it!" It is hard for us to understand that pure pleasure was created "very good." And it is hard for us to understand how pleasure is being recreated by Jesus as "very, very good."

INNOCENT PLEASURES

In a novel by Patrick O'Brian, a man considers

whether to buy an Amati violin. He loves music, but the violin is costly. His friend says to him, "Certainly you must have your fiddle. Any innocent pleasure is a real good: there are not so many of them."[2] In other words, "This is something truly good. Do it. Spend the money."

What gives *you* pure and simple pleasure? What truly refreshes you? What helps you to lay your cares down and get a fresh perspective on life? What enables you to step back into the business and hardship of life with a new joy?

My own list includes lighting up when I see an old friend – I'm so glad to see someone I love. A particular meal can evoke warm memories that take me back to childhood joys. And for simple pleasure, there is nothing finer than shooting hoops. One time I hit forty-seven straight free throws!

Sex should be on the list of pure pleasures. In our society, sex gets a bad name. But in the Bible, sex within marriage is an unstained, erotic joy. God made it, so it was good. It's the same thing with enjoying a good meal. In our society food takes on ugly and false meanings: Salvation? Poison? Fat calories? Escape? But it does not need to mean these things. We can say, "Thank you, God, for daily bread."

The Psalms revel in creation. We marvel at the unparalleled beauty of a sunrise and sunset, and even more at a Master Artist so creative that he will erase his art every day to begin again the next.

So many simple, unstained pleasures: Collecting stones on a lakeshore. Watching autumn leaves drop. These innocent pleasures are a means to step out of what is hard, painful, or difficult in our lives into something more beautiful.

What makes these pleasures innocent? It is the fact that there is a greatest pleasure, and that *greatest* pleasure is the Maker of all the innocent ones. Perhaps devotion to that God is one of your innocent pleasures. Perhaps pure pleasure comes to you in worship, through certain hymns or the celebration of the Lord's Supper. Whenever I read the Gospel of Luke, I rejoice in its picture of the tenderness of Jesus with the broken of the earth. The innocent pleasures come because the greatest pleasure – God himself – is in his rightful place.

Innocent pleasures don't pretend to save you or protect you. They don't promise you meaning and identity in life. They don't take life's fragility, pain, frustration, disappointment, and uncertainty and wash them away. They are not the giver of every good and perfect gift; they are just gifts you enjoy. They are innocent because they don't pretend to be anything more.

GUILTY PLEASURES

By contrast, which pleasures leave a residue, an oily stain? Which entertainments contain a quality of obsession, residual guilt, or anxiety? Which recreations bring disappointment? Which amusements tend to hijack you, promising to make you feel good, but then failing?

Stained and guilty pleasures often arise as a restless escape from troubles. Something in life is hard and we want a break. They promise good things but never deliver them. Instead, they leave you with queasy feelings.

What difficulties tempt you towards the guilty pleasures? There seem to be three broad categories:

4

- You are bored, lonely, with nothing to do.
- You are stressed, frustrated and worn out.
- You are hurt, betrayed, and treated unfairly. Perhaps you've lost someone or something you loved.

These tend to be the situations that lead you away from innocent pleasures to the stained and guilty ones. You grab for anything that will protect, soothe, comfort, or save you. This raises the crucial issue as we think about pleasure: *How do you face pain?* What do you do with it? To redeem pleasure, we need to answer this question.

TAKE HOLD OF SUFFERING

Scripture shows us that God runs his universe in ways that are counterintuitive. There is a counterintuitive door to the greatest pleasure, the one that makes the lesser, innocent pleasures bring joy in their proper place. That counterintuitive door is to face your suffering, to take hold of it instead of seeking to escape it. To stop what you are doing and honestly say to God, "I'm all alone right now. I'm tired. I'm bored. I'm hurt. I'm worried and stressed. Help me!" This is the counterintuitive door into joy.

The worship of the Bible expresses two things to God: our pain and our pleasure. For example, one mode of the Old Testament sacrificial system is about guilt, need, suffering and hardship. We need cleansing and deliverance. The other kind of sacrifice expresses gratitude. We have been blessed, we have a harvest, we are feasting, and we enjoy peace. We bring to God our pain and our pleasure.

Some psalms suffer honestly: "O God, I am in anguish. Deliver me from my sufferings and my sins." Other psalms delight honestly: "O my God, you are good. I thank you, worship you, and adore you." We speak both of our pain and pleasure. Somehow, in the way God runs his universe, our willingness to enter into the experience of pain, disappointment, loneliness, hurt, and stress – being willing to face it and not bolt for some lesser pleasure – winds up being the door to the greatest pleasure of all. And with the best come the other true pleasures, felt deeply.

In 1 Peter 1, affliction is the context of our entrance into "joy inexpressible and full of glory." In James 1, trial is the context of purpose, endurance, meaning, and joy. In Romans 5, we are told that "we exult in our tribulations," life's sorrows, anguish, misery, and pain. Paul says that we rejoice in the midst of our sufferings, *knowing* that "the love of God has been poured out within our hearts through the Holy Spirit who was given to us" (v. 5). Walking into suffering with our eyes wide open, and not running after escapist pleasures, is what opens the door to a knowledge of the love of God.

In *The Great Divorce*, C. S. Lewis describes how we humans typically misunderstand this. "They say of some temporal suffering [some moment of pain, loss, or betrayal], 'No future bliss can make up for it,' not knowing that Heaven, once attained, will work backwards and turn even that agony into a glory. And of some sinful pleasure they say, 'Let me have but *this* and I'll take the consequences': little dreaming how damnation will spread back

6

and back into their past and contaminate the pleasure of the sin. Both processes begin even before death. The good man's past begins to change so that his forgiven sins and remembered sorrows take on the quality of Heaven: the bad man's past already conforms to his badness and is filled only with dreariness."[3] Lewis is pointing out that the greatest pleasure works back even into our greatest sorrows, and they become doors to the pleasures that last forever.

In her hymn, "Be Still, My Soul," Katarina von Schlegel expressed great sorrow, yet a spring of life and joy wells up in the pain.

> Be still, my soul: the Lord is on thy side;
> bear patiently the cross of grief or pain;
> leave to thy God to order and provide;
> in every change, he faithful will remain.
> Be still, my soul; thy best, thy heav'nly
> Friend through thorny ways leads to a
> joyful end.

Katerina Von Schlegel understood that suffering tests whether our pleasure and hope are firmly attached to the one greatest pleasure, with the innocent pleasures following behind. The Episcopal Prayer of General Thanksgiving says, "We bless thee for our creation, preservation, and all the blessings of this life." We might paraphrase this, "We thank you for the innocent pleasures and the good things." But then this wise prayer goes on, "But above all [we thank thee] for thine inestimable love in the redemption of the world by our Lord Jesus Christ; for the means of grace, and for the hope of glory."[4] In the hands of a loving

God, sorrow and suffering become doorways into the greatest and most indestructible joys.

RECOGNIZING THE STAINED PLEASURES

What are the stained and guilty pleasures? Non-Christians often say, "I don't want to become a Christian because I'll have to give up the ten things I most love doing and do the ten things I most hate doing." These people don't realize that the things on their list are false. They don't understand how pleasure is truly wired into human experience.

What are the guilty pleasures in your life? The obvious ones would be immorality, anger, self-righteousness, gluttony, sloth and the like. But what about the things that are, in and of themselves, okay? They are good – or at least not bad. Yet they can capture your heart and become too important in your life. What is on your list of potentially innocent pleasures that go bad?

What about this list? Browsing a catalog. Checking email many times a day. Talking on the phone. How about reading novels – even good ones? It could be games or puzzles, talk radio, shopping or snacks between meals. There is nothing wrong with these activities in themselves. So how can you tell when a pleasure crosses the line from innocent to guilty? There are five warning signs.

The Pleasure Is Plain Wrong
The activity is sinful in and of itself. This includes drunkenness, lust, outbursts of anger, and gossip. These are the easy ones to spot.

8

The Pleasure Captures You

The activity is not sinful, but you become preoccupied with it. You obsess and fantasize about it. You can't wait to do it or have it. I remember driving to a conference when I suddenly realized that I'd been fantasizing about the Coke I would drink on the way home. I thought, *I seriously need to get a life!* There is nothing wrong with what I wanted to do, but why was my mind parked there? It was a minor stained pleasure. It took up too much mental space. It became too important.

Soon those pleasures don't just take mental space; they require action. You become compulsive about it. Every time you are bored and lonely, you flip on the TV. Every time you feel hurt or stressed out, you eat. It owns you. It masters you.

Every human being is obsessive-compulsive. OCD is not a diagnosis – it's a description of humanity. Obsession means that something is too much on our minds; compulsion means that something is too much in our actions. It leads to a stain. Paul says, "All things are lawful for me, but not all things are profitable…. I will not be mastered by anything" (1 Cor. 6:12).

The Pleasure Is Hidden

This is a real tip-off. It may be an innocent thing to do, but you hide it. Why? When you create a secret garden of any sort in your life, mutant things always grow. They start out as beautiful roses but they turn ugly when they grow in secret. Everything should be open to inspection, because in fact they are always seen by someone. There are no secrets before the Lord.

The Pleasure Steals You Away from the Good

A guilty pleasure steals you away from the good things you ought to be doing. You should call your sister but you read magazines for two hours. You should pay your bills but you check email. The bills start to clutter up tomorrow's schedule, and eventually this affects relationships. You're distracted and edgy, and you fail to love. It affects your job and your family.

The Pleasure Doesn't Deliver

Stained pleasures are often subtle. We don't always realize that we did something because it seemed to promise some sort of joy, satisfaction, refuge, or meaning. But stained pleasures never deliver. They leave you empty, anxious, guilty, more obsessed, and vaguely unhappy. You have to pull these guilty pleasures into the daylight to see them for what they are.

THE JOY LEVER

Watch an elderly woman get exquisite pleasure from the sunbeam on the kitchen floor, or a well-brewed cup of tea. A grandchild brings even greater joy. It takes less and less innocent pleasure to push the lever of joy. It's one of those secrets of the Christian life. Far from the belief that Christians have to give up everything they enjoy to do dreary things instead, the truth is that your pleasure mechanism is rearranged, giving you the freedom to feel all sorts of exquisite joys you never imagined. It takes less and less effort.

In the stained pleasure cycle, the addictive cycle, it takes more and more to push the lever of joy. Quoting again from *The Great Divorce*, "The sensualist… begins by pursuing a real pleasure, though a small one…. But the time comes on when, though the pleasure becomes less and less and the craving fiercer and fiercer, and though he knows that joy can never come that way, yet he prefers to joy the mere fondling of unappeasable lust and would not have it taken from him. He'd fight to the death to keep it. He'd like well to be able to scratch: but even when he can scratch no more he'd rather itch than not."[5]

Stained pleasures have this corroding effect. They always up the ante. You watch more movies and listen to more music. You exercise harder and longer. You think, *This video game isn't graphic enough. That vacation isn't exotic enough. This pornography isn't explicit enough. This amount of alcohol isn't enough.* The pleasures dull and sometimes completely disappear. We get no satisfaction from eating, yet we shovel food into our mouths anyway. The drunken person becomes somber and unhappy. The high from marijuana brings paranoid terror. The thrill of these guilty pleasures is gone.

What is it like for you to push the lever of joy? Is it becoming harder and harder or easier and easier? Let me suggest two small but significant action plans to move in the right direction. The first aims to cultivate innocent pleasures. The second aims to remove the stains that pervert pleasure.

Action Plan 1: Stop… and Enjoy Yourself

If you are the sort of person who dutifully presses on through life, take a break from your busyness. Step off the treadmill of duties at work, home, and church.

If you are the sort of person who rushes into recreation, take a break from your exercise, TV, hobbies, movies, video games, snacking, phone calls, and whatever.

Whether you live to work or live to play, stop to think about something very important.

• In your experience, what has proved *truly restful?*

• What has left you feeling *nourished* afterwards?

Think about this yourself, then talk it over with people close to you. Stick to the small everyday things that don't take lots of time, effort, and money. What are the things you linger to appreciate, that give you a good, hearty laugh, that leave you encouraged, or help you sleep? What tasks lead you to savor the achievement and give thanks to God? These innocent pleasures may involve your children, nature, exercise, music, or worship. Do you build joys such as these?

Second, what pleasures leave no residue, no guilt, exhaustion, or unrest? This can be a very revealing question. Do the things you do instinctively leave you refreshed or more restless? Compare the things you turn to for "a break" with the things that actually bring delight. God *made* us for rest and pleasure, and he wired us so that stained pleasures will leave a stain, and the innocent pleasures are pure pleasure.

Third, what is the invigorating opposite of your workaday life? If you're a landscaper, sit down and read a good book. If you're a scholar, go and work in the garden. If you're a stay-at-home mom, arrange for someone to care for the kids. If you put in long hours at the office, take care of the kids. You get the idea. Honest work and honest rest are complementary goods. The Bible's view of rest ("sabbath") is not legalistic; it's restful and refreshing. And since God tailor-makes everyone different, what's deeply pleasurable will vary from one person to the next.

Action Plan 2: Take a One-Week Fast

What forms of pleasure do you pursue impulsively or compulsively? I'm not talking about sinful pleasures like immorality, gossip, and drunkenness. I'm talking about potentially innocent ones that tend to run out of control. Do you look forward *too much* to that cup of coffee, that phone call, or that book? Do you jump into it *too automatically?* Then take a one-week break.

Perhaps that doesn't sound like much; perhaps it sounds impossible! Either way, view it as a holy experiment. An intentional fast from your recreation habits works against obsessive pleasure-seeking and teaches you fascinating things about yourself and your God.

What will happen when you fast?

First, you will struggle. You will start to think, *"I want to do it, I need to do it. I can't give this up."* You discover the power of the desire when you try to give it up. This simple thing has power over you!

Second, you will think, *"If I don't do it, I'll be bored"* – or hurt, or stressed. You will face the difficulty and trouble of life.

Third, you will realize that even in this small, insignificant part of life, you need Jesus' help and mercy. You really do. You realize how strong the lusts are. You recognize the nature of the sufferings

13

and difficulties of life and how you've been medicating yourself by your little guilty pleasure. You realize that you need help. And Jesus is the One who says, "Come to me and I will give you grace to help you in your time of need."

Fourth, you gain an increased awareness of other people because you aren't numbing yourself with pleasures that control your mind, time, and actions. You discover innocent pleasures that have more life to them. You think, *I don't need to eat compulsively. I can watch the leaves drop off the maple tree. I can do something for a friend.* Your joy and sense of purpose increase. You think more clearly. A tiny change can make a big difference. It takes less and less to push the lever of joy in your life.

THE DEEP PLEASURES

What are the supreme pleasures? God and people. The commandments tell us to love God and love our neighbor. In so doing, they don't just convict us of sin and tell us what to do. They drive us to the Christ who perfectly fulfilled them, and then they lay out the pathway to the most supreme joy imaginable.

Psalm 23 is an expression of the supreme pleasure of knowing the Lord.

> The LORD is my shepherd,
> I shall not want.
> He makes me lie down in green pastures;
> He leads me beside quiet waters.
> He restores my soul;
> He guides me in the paths of righteousness
> for his name's sake.

14

Even though I walk through the valley of
the shadow of death,
I fear no evil, for you are with me;
Your rod and your staff, they comfort me.
You prepare a table before me in the
presence of my enemies;
You have anointed my head with oil;
My cup overflows.
Surely goodness and lovingkindness will
follow me all the days of my life,
And I will dwell in the house of the LORD
forever.

Notice how the psalmist takes hold of suffering.
He looks the shadow of death right in the eye. "I
fear no evil, for you are with me." Notice, too, how
he switches from talking about God in the third
person ("he") to the second person ("you") in an
amazing expression of intimacy with God. In the
last image, the psalmist is saying that goodness and
lovingkindness are literally chasing him! "I am
being pursued by your goodness and lovingkindness
all my life, and then I will live with you forever."
This is the supreme pleasure.

The psalmist invites us to personalize this psalm
for ourselves and enter into this same intimacy.

You, O Lord, Savior, King, and Master,
are my shepherd. I lack nothing.

You make my soul rest in places of
beauty, peace, safety, and pure pleasure.

You turn me back to you – you bring
me back to what life is really all about.

You guide me in the paths of
righteousness; every wrong made

right, every suffering made joy, every sin made righteousness. You guide me in those paths for your name's sake; it is because of who you are that you do this.

Even in the hard times, I will fear no evil. You are here to comfort and protect me. You provide for me richly, no matter what the circumstances.

You pour blessing on my head and make my cup overflow. It is a certainty that your goodness and unchanging love will follow me all through my life.

And then I will be with you forever, living in your presence.

One step behind the supreme pleasure of loving God is the pleasure of true friendship – loving others. We sometimes get confused about the fact that there are people we deeply enjoy. We've all heard that *agape* love is an act of the will, contrary to how we feel. We know that the Bible tells us that we shouldn't just hang out with our friends. We should reach out to people who are different from us, to the stranger, and even to our enemies. We might start to think that the paradigm for relationships is, *To really love people, I should associate with people I don't like; with people who are tough to get along with, manipulative, neurotic, high maintenance, awkward and aggressive – people who require a lot of effort!* But something is wrong with that view. You say, "I really like these other people! They are my friends, people I respect. They love me and help me. Does that mean I *shouldn't* pursue people if we care about each other?" That can't be it!

The Bible holds these two pictures of relationship in tension. The leading theme, the richer theme, involves the people you truly enjoy. Here we talk about my beloved brother, my sister, my wife, the child I hold in my arms, my dear friend. In heaven we will see face to face the One we love, the supreme Person. But heaven is also a place full of other relationships you enjoy. These people love you without pretense, competition, or manipulation.

Side by side with that call to joyous intimacy is a call to get out of your comfort zone. The harder call of the Bible is to love our enemies, to love strangers and people who are different from you – needy, sinful, broken people. This call comes for two reasons. First, it tests whether you are turning the innocent pleasures of intimacy into a stained pleasure. Are the people you like turning into a clique?

Second, the call tests whether we are willing to widen the circle of intimacy so that enemies become friends, strangers become like family, and someone I don't know becomes like my dear sister. The goal is always the simple, joyous relationship with others – the affection and the give-and-take. But this is a call to widen your circle of friendship, to avoid making gods out of those who bring you the greatest pleasure. Ultimately every child of the Most High will be greeted by others who light up when they see us.

THE REDEMPTION OF PLEASURE

The well-loved hymn, "Fairest Lord Jesus," portrays the redemption of pleasure as we enter into worship of the glorious, beautiful, adorable Christ.

Fairest Lord Jesus, Ruler of all nature,
Son of God and Son of Man!
Thee will I cherish, thee will I honor,
Thou, my soul's glory, joy, and crown.

Personalize this song and use it to enter into redeemed pleasure with your Lord.

Jesus, we worship and adore you. We thank you that heaven is all pleasure. There is no stain or compulsion. There are no disappointed hopes. Nothing is wrong! Nothing distracts us from what we ought to do. You created us, our Lord, to love you and to love each other, and to enjoy all the blessings of this life. Yet you do so in such a way that we are willing to go through suffering and wrestle with our own sinfulness, to look at the way we corrupt what is intended for good. We thank you, Father, for Jesus Christ, who forgives, who lives as the Man of joy. We thank you that Jesus was willing to embrace suffering, as he entered into our struggle with sinfulness and took the wrath that is our due. We thank you that Jesus Christ is now seated at the right hand of God, his work complete. And we look forward to seeing your face, our Lord and King, the fairest of the fair, Lord Jesus.
Amen.

NOTES

[1] Neil Postman, *Amusing Ourselves to Death: Public Discourse in the Age of Show Business* (New York: Penguin Books, 1985), vii-viii.

[2] Patrick O'Brian, *Post Captain* (New York: W. W. Norton, 1972), p. 60.

[3] C. S. Lewis, *The Great Divorce* (New York: HarperCollins, 1946), pp. 67-68.

[4] *Book of Common Prayer* (New York: Oxford University Press, 1935), p. 19.

[5] C. S. Lewis, *The Great Divorce*, p. 70.

David Powlison, M.Div., Ph.D.,

Dr. Powlison edits *The Journal of Biblical Counseling,* counsels and teaches in CCEF's School of Biblical Counseling, and teaches Practical Theology at Westminster Theological Seminary. He has written *Power Encounters: Reclaiming Spiritual Warfare; Competent to Counsel?: The History of a Conservative Protestant Anti-Psychiatry Movement; Seeing with New Eyes: Counseling and the Human Condition Through the Lens of Scripture* and numerous articles on counseling. David and his wife, Nan, have a son and two daughters.

Other Booklets by Our Authors